PENGUIN BOOKS
Poems of Thomas Hardy

Thomas Hardy (1840–1928) was an English poet, short-story writer and novelist. The son of a stonemason, he was born in Dorset. He was apprenticed to a local architect, and found initial success with *Far From the Madding Crowd* (1874). The same year he married Emma Gifford. Among his most famous works are *The Return of the Native* (1878), *The Mayor of Casterbridge* (1886) and *Tess of the D'Ubervilles* (1891).

Claire Tomalin worked in publishing and journalism for many years. She was literary editor of the *New Statesman* and the *Sunday Times*, before devoting herself to writing full time. She is the author of seven highly acclaimed biographies: *The Life and Death of Mary Wollstonecraft*, which won the Whitbread First Book Prize; *Shelley and his World*; *Katherine Mansfield: A Secret Life*, *The Invisible Woman: The Story of Nelly Ternan*; *Charles Dickens*, which won the Hawthornden Prize, the NCR Book Award and the James Tait Black Memorial Prize for Biography; *Mrs Jordan's Profession*; *Jane Austen: A Life*; and *Samuel Pepys: The Unequalled Self*, which was 2002 Whitbread Book of the Year. Her acclaimed biography of Hardy, *Thomas Hardy: The Time-Torn Man*, is now available in paperback.

Poems of
Thomas Hardy

*Selected and with an Introduction
by* CLAIRE TOMALIN

PENGUIN BOOKS

PENGUIN BOOKS

Published by the Penguin Group
Penguin Books Ltd, 80 Strand, London WC2R ORL, England
Penguin Group (USA) Inc., 375 Hudson Street, New York 10014, USA
Penguin Group (Canada), 90 Eglinton Avenue East, Suite 700, Toronto, Ontario, Canada M4P 2Y3
(a division of Pearson Penguin Canada Inc.)
Penguin Ireland, 25 St Stephen's Green, Dublin 2, Ireland (a division of Penguin Books Ltd)
Penguin Group (Australia), 250 Camberwell Road,
Camberwell, Victoria 3124, Australia (a division of Pearson Australia Group Pty Ltd)
Penguin Books India Pvt Ltd, 11 Community Centre,
Panchsheel Park, New Delhi – 110 017, India
Penguin Group (NZ), 67 Apollo Drive, Rosedale, North Shore 0632, New Zealand
(a division of Pearson New Zealand Ltd)
Penguin Books (South Africa) (Pty) Ltd, 24 Sturdee Avenue,
Rosebank, Johannesburg 2196, South Africa

Penguin Books Ltd, Registered Offices: 80 Strand, London WC2R ORL, England

www.penguin.com

This selection first published 2006
Published as a Penguin Red Classic 2007
I

Selection and introduction copyright © Claire Tomalin, 2006
All rights reserved

Printed in England by Clays Ltd, St Ives plc

Except in the United States of America, this book is sold subject
to the condition that it shall not, by way of trade or otherwise, be lent,
re-sold, hired out, or otherwise circulated without the publisher's
prior consent in any form of binding or cover other than that in
which it is published and without a similar condition including this
condition being imposed on the subsequent purchaser

ISBN: 978-0-140-42471-3

Contents

Home and Family

These are poems about Hardy's parents' wooing, the history and setting of the cottage at Higher Bockhampton, his early childhood and his sister Mary.

The Young Man

Poems known to have been written in London in the 1860s and 70s, possibly revised later.

Weather, Birds, Beasts

Journeys

The drama of travel, roads and railways, caught Hardy's imagination, but his only poem about a sea crossing is the magnificent account of the Titanic, *one of the very few poems he wrote to order.*

Marriage

Poems written during his first marriage, describing an early quarrel, happy times, a tender look at his ageing wife and an unhappy account of being unable to revive his early feelings for her, written forty years after their first meeting.

Love in Middle Age

Hardy alternated between turning his back on love and suffering torments of longing. He describes meeting Mrs Florence Henniker in town, and another occasion when she stood him up. The last poem is about Florence Dugdale, who became his second wife.

Remembering Emma
From Poems of 1912–1913 – *Veteris vestigia flammae*

These are from the sequence inspired by the death of his first wife. He said that the shock, grief and remorse for their long estrangement put him 'in flower' as a poet, and he wrote faster and more freely than he had ever done.

More about Emma

He continued to write about Emma for the rest of his life, revisiting their past in minute detail.

War

Hardy wrote about four wars, first the Napoleonic wars which he studied obsessively. The Franco–Prussian war of 1870 inspired the last of this group, although the poem was not finished until 1915. The Boer War killed the Dorset boy of 'The Dead Drummer', and World War I was foreseen in 'Channel Firing' and lamented in 'The Pity of It'.

On Himself

Hardy mythologized himself and gave humorous and critical accounts of his own behaviour, celebrated his love of music, and reflected on his own approaching death, sometimes apprehensively, more often with the tranquillity of one who was content to return to the earth in a country churchyard.

People and Stories

Leslie Stephen, editor and man of letters, was a friend whose favourite pursuit was climbing in the Alps. Hardy was inspired for his poem about Keats by reading that his last moments on English soil came when he went ashore in Dorset, probably at Lulworth Cove. The third poem is a surreal account of a family, probably Emma's, moving house. The three final poems concentrate human stories into a few lines – a reminder that he was also a novelist with an eye for a plot.

Introduction

Hardy's chief subject as a poet was his own experience, and although he also wrote narrative verse this selection concentrates on poems that mythologize his life, the people he loved and the places to which he responded most deeply. After years of writing novels to earn his living – novels which contain seams of poetry, but in which he felt constrained to work to the demands of the market – poetry came to him as a relief and a pleasure, and as a chief he sometimes gives the impression of a man who was continually unfolding and turning about his past like a map, and alighting on half-forgotten spots which suddenly become vivid to him. Poetry also allowed him to speak with a raw intensity: 'I Look Into My Glass' is about sexual longing, 'Who's in the Next Room?' about the terror of death, 'Penance' about the horror or remorse that comes when it is too late to put things right. These are powerful poems, but he does not impose his personality on the reader, simply reports. His presence is quiet even when his message is harrowing.

He was essentially a lyric poet, working a great deal in his head, I guess, before he put anything down, although it has come to light that he sometimes plotted out the shapes of poems on paper. He told Robert Graves he never made more than four drafts, and there is always an element of song around what Philip Larkin called 'the little spinal cord of thought'. It reminds us that he grew up hearing ballads sung by country people and dancing to music played at home on the violin by his father, who taught him to play alongside him. Music ran in the family, and by the time he was a schoolboy he was going out with his father and uncle to make music for weddings and parties around the local villages. And as Thom Gunn pointed out, he also absorbed and used the devices of the ballad, particularly the unexplained voice that speaks or questions mysteriously.

No one wanted to publish his early poems but he kept writing verse during the three decades in which he worked as a novelist, always considering himself primarily a poet. His first collection, *Wessex Poems*, came out in 1898, when he was nearly sixty, and he was seventy-two when the death of his first wife Emma, from whom he had been long estranged, inspired him to his most concentrated and remarkable burst of poems. This was in 1912 and 1913, when he described himself as being 'in flower' as a poet, and it is one of the most surprising moments in English poetry.

He started writing poetry as a young man and continued until a few hours before his death, when he dictated some last lines. About a thousand poems are known, many impossible to date because he kept his early manuscripts and reworked them at different times, and all his eight collections mix old and new work. Sometimes he put a date or a place under the title or at the end, more often not.

Hardy was extremely well read in the Latin and Greek poets as well as the English, Shakespeare, the Romantics, Scott, Tennyson, Browning, Swinburne and his fellow Dorset poet William Barnes, and he wrote in a tradition that valued formal structure. But his voice is entirely his own, with its gnarled usages, its compound words – 'wind-warped', 'spectre-grey', 'ghost-girl-rider', 'dew-dashed', its wonderful images like the reflections of the hands, 'growing paler and paler', belonging to the generations of women who have polished the family furniture; like the stars closing their shutters in the whitening dawn; or 'the original air-blue gown' of the once beloved girl. He did not repeat himself, and almost every poem has something unexpected in it. His reputation has grown steadily and he is admired by both traditionalists and modernists. Donald Davie, writing in 1973, claimed that he had been the most far-reaching influence on British poetry over the previous fifty years, more than Yeats, Eliot, Pound or Lawrence.

Claire Tomalin

Home and Family

A Church Romance
(Mellstock: circa 1835)

She turned in the high pew, until her sight
Swept the west gallery, and caught its row
Of music-men with viol, book, and bow
Against the sinking sad tower-window light.

She turned again; and in her pride's despite
One strenuous viol's inspirer seemed to throw
A message from his string to her below,
Which said: 'I claim thee as my own forthright!'

Thus their hearts' bond began, in due time signed.
And long years thence, when Age had scared
                                    Romance,
At some old attitude of his or glance
That gallery-scene would break upon her mind,
With him as minstrel, ardent, young, and trim,
Bowing 'New Sabbath' or 'Mount Ephraim.'

Heredity

I am the family face;
Flesh perishes, I live on,
Projecting trait and trace
Through time to times anon,
And leaping from place to place
Over oblivion.

The years-heired feature that can
In curve and voice and eye
Despise the human span
Of durance – that is I;
The eternal thing in man,
That heeds no call to die.

Domicilium

It faces west, and round the back and sides
High beeches, bending, hang a veil of boughs,
And sweep against the roof. Wild honeysucks
Climb on the walls, and seem to sprout a wish
(If we may fancy wish of trees and plants)
To overtop the apple-trees hard by.

Red roses, lilacs, variegated box
Are there in plenty, and such hardy flowers
As flourish best untrained. Adjoining these
Are herbs and esculents; and farther still
A field; then cottages with trees, and last
The distant hills and sky.

Behind, the scene is wilder. Heath and furze
Are everything that seems to grow and thrive
Upon the uneven ground. A stunted thorn
Stands here and there, indeed; and from a pit
An oak uprises, springing from a seed
Dropped by some bird a hundred years ago.

                              In days bygone –
Long gone – my father's mother, who is now
Blest with the blest, would take me out to walk.
At such a time I once inquired of her
How looked the spot when first she settled here.
The answer I remember. 'Fifty years
Have passed since then, my child, and change has
                                        marked
The face of all things. Yonder garden-plots

5

And orchards were uncultivated slopes
O'ergrown with bramble bushes, furze and thorn:
That road a narrow path shut in by ferns,
Which, almost trees, obscured the passer-by.

'Our house stood quite alone, and those tall firs
And beeches were not planted. Snakes and efts
Swarmed in the summer days, and nightly bats
Would fly about our bedrooms. Heathcroppers
Lived on the hills, and were our only friends;
So wild it was when first we settled here.'

The Self-Unseeing

Here is the ancient floor,
Footworn and hollowed and thin,
Here was the former door
Where the dead feet walked in.

She sat here in her chair,
Smiling into the fire;
He who played stood there,
Bowing it higher and higher.

Childlike, I danced in a dream;
Blessings emblazoned that day;
Everything glowed with a gleam;
Yet we were looking away!

The Roman Road

The Roman Road runs straight and bare
As the pale parting-line in hair
Across the heath. And thoughtful men
Contrast its days of Now and Then,
And delve, and measure, and compare;

Visioning on the vacant air
Helmed legionaries, who proudly rear
The Eagle, as they pace again
                    The Roman Road.

But no tall brass-helmed legionnaire
Haunts it for me. Uprises there
A mother's form upon my ken,
Guiding my infant steps, as when
We walked that ancient thoroughfare,
                    The Roman Road.

Logs on the Hearth
A Memory of a Sister

The fire advances along the log
      Of the tree we felled,
Which bloomed and bore striped apples by the
                        peck
   Till its last hour of bearing knelled.

The fork that first my hand would reach
      And then my foot
In climbings upward inch by inch, lies now
   Sawn, sapless, darkening with soot.

Where the bark chars is where, one year,
      It was pruned, and bled –
Then overgrew the wound. But now, at last,
   Its growings all have stagnated.

My fellow-climber rises dim
      From her chilly grave –
Just as she was, her foot near mine on the
                  bending limb,
   Laughing, her young brown hand awave.

December 1915

Old Furniture

I know not how it may be with others
    Who sit amid relics of householdry
That date from the days of their mothers'
                      mothers,
    But well I know how it is with me
      Continually.

I see the hands of the generations
    That owned each shiny familiar thing
In play on its knobs and indentations,
    And with its ancient fashioning
      Still dallying:

Hands behind hands, growing paler and paler,
    As in a mirror a candle-flame
Shows images of itself, each frailer
    As it recedes, though the eye may frame
      Its shape the same.

On the clock's dull dial a foggy finger,
    Moving to set the minutes right
With tentative touches that lift and linger
    In the wont of a moth on a summer night,
      Creeps to my sight.

On this old viol, too, fingers are dancing –
    As whilom – just over the strings by the nut,
The tip of a bow receding, advancing
    In airy quivers, as if it would cut
      The plaintive gut.

And I see a face by that box for tinder,
    Glowing forth in fits from the dark,
And fading again, as the linten cinder
    Kindles to red at the flinty spark,
        Or goes out stark.

Well, well. It is best to be up and doing,
    The world has no use for one to-day
Who eyes things thus – no aim pursuing!
    He should not continue in this stay,
        But sink away.

Four in the Morning

At four this day of June I rise:
The dawn-light strengthens steadily;
Earth is a cerule mystery,
As if not far from Paradise
              At four o'clock,

Or else near the Great Nebula,
Or where the Pleiads blink and smile:
(For though we see with eyes of guile
The grisly grin of things by day,
              At four o'clock

They show their best.) . . . In this vale's space
I am up the first, I think. Yet, no,
A whistling? and the to-and-fro
Wheezed whettings of a scythe apace
              At four o'clock? . . .

– Though pleasure spurred, I rose with irk:
Here is one at compulsion's whip
Taking his life's stern stewardship
With blithe uncare, and hard at work
              At four o'clock!

Bockhampton

The Young Man

A Young Man's Exhortation

Call off your eyes from care
By some determined deftness; put forth joys
Dear as excess without the core that cloys,
    And charm Life's lourings fair.

Exalt and crown the hour
That girdles us, and fill it full with glee,
Blind glee, excelling aught could ever be
    Were heedfulness in power.

Send up such touching strains
That limitless recruits from Fancy's pack
Shall rush upon your tongue, and tender back
    All that your soul contains.

For what do we know best?
That a fresh love-leaf crumpled soon will dry,
And that men moment after moment die,
    Of all scope dispossest.

If I have seen one thing
It is the passing preciousness of dreams;
That aspects are within us; and who seems
    Most kingly is the King.

1867: Westbourne Park Villas

The Ruined Maid

'O 'melia, my dear, this does everything crown!
Who could have supposed I should meet you in
                                        Town?
And whence such fair garments, such prosperi-ty?' –
'O didn't you know I'd been ruined?' said she.

– 'You left us in tatters, without shoes or socks,
Tired of digging potatoes, and spudding up docks;
And now you've gay bracelets and bright feathers
                                        three!' –
'Yes: that's how we dress when we're ruined,' said she.

– 'At home in the barton you said "thee" and "thou,"
And "thik oon," and "theäs oon," and "t'other"; but
                                                now
Your talking quite fits 'ee for high compa-ny!' –
'Some polish is gained with one's ruin,' said she.

– 'Your hands were like paws then, your face blue and
                                                bleak
But now I'm bewitched by your delicate cheek,
And your little gloves fit as on any la-dy!' –
'We never do work when we're ruined,' said she.

– 'You used to call home-life a hag-ridden dream,
And you'd sigh, and you'd sock; but at present you
                                                seem
To know not of megrims or melancho-ly!' –
'True. One's pretty lively when ruined,' said she.

– 'I wish I had feathers, a fine sweeping gown,
And a delicate face, and could strut about Town!' –
'My dear – a raw country girl, such as you be,
Cannot quite expect that. You ain't ruined,' said she.

Westbourne Park Villas, 1866

Neutral Tones

We stood by a pond that winter day,
And the sun was white, as though chidden of God,
And a few leaves lay on the starving sod;
     – They had fallen from an ash, and were gray.

Your eyes on me were as eyes that rove
Over tedious riddles of years ago;
And some words played between us to and fro
     On which lost the more by our love.

The smile on your mouth was the deadest thing
Alive enough to have strength to die;
And a grin of bitterness swept thereby
     Like an ominous bird a-wing. . . .

Since then, keen lessons that love deceives,
And wrings with wrong, have shaped to me
Your face, and the God-curst sun, and a tree,
     And a pond edged with grayish leaves.

1867

Coming up Oxford Street: Evening

The sun from the west glares back,
And the sun from the watered track,
And the sun from the sheets of glass,
And the sun from each window-brass;
Sun-mirrorings, too, brighten
From show-cases beneath
The laughing eyes and teeth
Of ladies who rouge and whiten.
And the same warm god explores
Panels and chinks of doors;
Problems with chymists' bottles
Profound as Aristotle's
He solves, and with good cause,
Having been ere man was.

Also he dazzles the pupils of one who walks west,
A city-clerk, with eyesight not of the best,
Who sees no escape to the very verge of his days
From the rut of Oxford Street into open ways;
And he goes along with head and eyes flagging forlorn,
Empty of interest in things, and wondering why he was
born.

As seen July 4, 1872

Weather, Birds, Beasts

Weathers

I

This is the weather the cuckoo likes,
    And so do I;
When showers betumble the chestnut spikes,
    And nestlings fly:
And the little brown nightingale bills his best,
And they sit outside at 'The Travellers' Rest,'
And maids come forth sprig-muslin drest,
And citizens dream of the south and west,
    And so do I.

II

This is the weather the shepherd shuns,
    And so do I;
When beeches drip in browns and duns,
    And thresh, and ply;
And hill-hid tides throb, throe on throe,
And meadow rivulets overflow,
And drops on gate-bars hang in a row,
And rooks in families homeward go,
    And so do I.

Snow in the Suburbs

Every branch big with it,
  Bent every twig with it;
Every fork like a white web-foot;
Every street and pavement mute:
Some flakes have lost their way, and grope back
                              upward, when
Meeting those meandering down they turn and
                              descend again.
  The palings are glued together like a wall,
  And there is no waft of wind with the fleecy fall.

  A sparrow enters the tree,
    Whereon immediately
  A snow-lump thrice his own slight size
  Descends on him and showers his head and eyes,
    And overturns him,
    And near inurns him,
  And lights on a nether twig, when its brush
Starts off a volley of other lodging lumps with a rush.

  The steps are a blanched slope,
    Up which, with feeble hope,
  A black cat comes, wide-eyed and thin;
    And we take him in.

The Darkling Thrush

I leant upon a coppice gate
    When Frost was spectre-gray,
And Winter's dregs made desolate
    The weakening eye of day.
The tangled bine-stems scored the sky
    Like strings of broken lyres,
And all mankind that haunted nigh
    Had sought their household fires.

The land's sharp features seemed to be
    The Century's corpse outleant,
His crypt the cloudy canopy,
    The wind his death-lament.
The ancient pulse of germ and birth
    Was shrunken hard and dry,
And every spirit upon earth
    Seemed fervourless as I.

At once a voice arose among
    The bleak twigs overhead
In a full-hearted evensong
    Of joy illimited;
An aged thrush, frail, gaunt, and small,
    In blast-beruffled plume,
Had chosen thus to fling his soul
    Upon the growing gloom.

So little cause for carolings
    Of such ecstatic sound
Was written on terrestrial things
    Afar or nigh around,
That I could think there trembled through
    His happy good-night air
Some blessed Hope, whereof he knew
    And I was unaware.

31st December 1900

The Oxen

Christmas Eve, and twelve of the clock.
  'Now they are all on their knees,'
An elder said as we sat in a flock
  By the embers in hearthside ease.

We pictured the meek mild creatures where
  They dwelt in their strawy pen,
Nor did it occur to one of us there
  To doubt they were kneeling then.

So fair a fancy few would weave
  In these years! Yet, I feel,
If someone said on Christmas Eve,
  'Come; see the oxen kneel

'In the lonely barton by yonder coomb
  Our childhood used to know,'
I should go with him in the gloom,
  Hoping it might be so.

1915

An August Midnight

I

A shaded lamp and a waving blind,
And the beat of a clock from a distant floor:
On this scene enter – winged, horned, and spined –
A longlegs, a moth, and a dumbledore;
While 'mid my page there idly stands
A sleepy fly, that rubs its hands . . .

II

Thus meet we five, in this still place,
At this point of time, at this point in space.
– My guests besmear my new-penned line,
Or bang at the lamp and fall supine.
'God's humblest, they!' I muse. Yet why?
They know Earth-secrets that know not I.

Max Gate, 1899

At Day-Close in November

The ten hours' light is abating,
    And a late bird wings across,
Where the pines, like waltzers waiting,
    Give their black heads a toss.

Beech leaves, that yellow the noon-time,
    Float past like specks in the eye;
I set every tree in my June time,
    And now they obscure the sky.

And the children who ramble through here
    Conceive that there never has been
A time when no tall trees grew here,
    That none will in time be seen.

'I Watched a Blackbird'

I watched a blackbird on a budding sycamore
One Easter Day, when sap was stirring twigs to the core;
  I saw his tongue, and crocus-coloured bill
    Parting and closing as he turned his trill;
    Then he flew down, seized on a stem of hay,
And upped to where his building scheme was under way,
As if so sure a nest were never shaped on spray.

Proud Songsters

The thrushes sing as the sun is going,
    And the finches whistle in ones and pairs,
And as it gets dark loud nightingales
      In bushes
Pipe, as they can when April wears,
    As if all Time were theirs.

These are brand-new birds of twelve-months'
                  growing,
Which a year ago, or less than twain,
No finches were, nor nightingales,
      Nor thrushes,
But only particles of grain,
    And earth, and air, and rain.

Night-Time in Mid-Fall

It is a storm-strid night, winds footing swift
      Through the blind profound;
   I know the happenings from their sound;
Leaves totter down still green, and spin and drift;
The tree-trunks rock to their roots, which wrench
                           and lift
The loam where they run onward underground.

The streams are muddy and swollen; eels migrate
      To a new abode;
   Even cross, 'tis said, the turnpike-road;
(Men's feet have felt their crawl, home-coming late):
The westward fronts of towers are saturate,
Church-timbers crack, and witches ride abroad.

The Fallow Deer at the Lonely House

One without looks in to-night
    Through the curtain-chink
From the sheet of glistening white;
One without looks in to-night
        As we sit and think
        By the fender-brink.

We do not discern those eyes
    Watching in the snow;
Lit by lamps of rosy dyes
We do not discern those eyes
        Wondering, aglow,
        Fourfooted, tiptoe.

Journeys

Life and Death at Sunrise
(Near Dogbury Gate, 1867)

The hills uncap their tops
Of woodland, pasture, copse,
And look on the layers of mist
At their foot that still persist:
They are like awakened sleepers on one elbow lifted,
Who gaze around to learn if things during night have
shifted.

A waggon creaks up from the fog
With a laboured leisurely jog;
Then a horseman from off the hill-tip
Comes clapping down into the dip;
While woodlarks, finches, sparrows, try to entune at
one time,
And cocks and hens and cows and bulls take up the
chime.

With a shouldered basket and flagon
A man meets the one with the waggon,
And both the men halt of long use.
'Well,' the waggoner says, 'what's the news?'
'– 'Tis a boy this time. You've just met the doctor
trotting back.
She's doing very well. And we think we shall call
him "Jack."

'And what have you got covered there?'
He nods to the waggon and mare.
'Oh, a coffin for old John Thinn:
We are just going to put him in.'

'– So he's gone at last. He always had a good
constitution.'
'– He was ninety-odd. He could call up the French
Revolution.'

'When I set out for Lyonnesse'
(1870)

When I set out for Lyonnesse,
    A hundred miles away,
    The rime was on the spray,
And starlight lit my lonesomeness
When I set out for Lyonnesse
    A hundred miles away.

What would bechance at Lyonnesse
    While I should sojourn there
    No prophet durst declare,
Nor did the wisest wizard guess
What would bechance at Lyonnesse
    While I should sojourn there.

When I came back from Lyonnesse
    With magic in my eyes,
    All marked with mute surmise
My radiance rare and fathomless,
When I came back from Lyonnesse
    With magic in my eyes!

In a Waiting Room

On a morning sick as the day of doom
    With the drizzling gray
    Of an English May,
There were few in the railway waiting-room.
About its walls were framed and varnished
Pictures of liners, fly-blown, tarnished.
The table bore a Testament
For travellers' reading, if suchwise bent.

    I read it on and on,
And, thronging the Gospel of Saint John,
Were figures – additions, multiplications –
By some one scrawled, with sundry emendations;
    Not scoffingly designed,
    But with an absent mind, –
Plainly a bagman's counts of cost,
What he had profited, what lost;
And whilst I wondered if there could have been
    Any particle of a soul
    In that poor man at all,
    To cypher rates of wage
    Upon that printed page,
    There joined in the charmless scene
And stood over me and the scribbled book
    (To lend the hour's mean hue
    A smear of tragedy too)
A soldier and wife, with haggard look

Subdued to stone by strong endeavour;
    And then I heard
    From a casual word
They were parting as they believed for ever.

    But next there came
    Like the eastern flame
Of some high altar, children – a pair –
Who laughed at the fly-blown pictures there.
'Here are the lovely ships that we,
Mother, are by and by going to see!
When we get there it's 'most sure to be fine,
And the band will play, and the sun will shine!'
It rained on the skylight with a din
As we waited and still no train came in;
But the words of the child in the squalid room
Had spread a glory through the gloom.

At the Railway Station, Upway

'There is not much that I can do,
    For I've no money that's quite my own!'
    Spoke up the pitying child –
A little boy with a violin
At the station before the train came in, –
'But I can play my fiddle to you,
And a nice one 'tis, and good in tone!'

    The man in the handcuffs smiled;
The constable looked, and he smiled, too,
    As the fiddle began to twang;
And the man in the handcuffs suddenly sang
            With grimful glee:
            'This life so free
            Is the thing for me!'
And the constable smiled, and said no word,
As if unconscious of what he heard;
And so they went on till the train came in –
The convict, and boy with the violin.

Midnight on the Great Western

In the third-class seat sat the journeying boy,
    And the roof-lamp's oily flame
Played down on his listless form and face,
Bewrapt past knowing to what he was going,
    Or whence he came.

In the band of his hat the journeying boy
    Had a ticket stuck; and a string
Around his neck bore the key of his box,
That twinkled gleams of the lamp's sad beams
    Like a living thing.

What past can be yours, O journeying boy
    Towards a world unknown,
Who calmly, as if incurious quite
On all at stake, can undertake
    This plunge alone?

Knows your soul a sphere, O journeying boy,
    Our rude realms far above,
Whence with spacious vision you mark and mete
This region of sin that you find you in,
    But are not of?

Faintheart in a Railway Train

At nine in the morning there passed a church,
At ten there passed me by the sea,
At twelve a town of smoke and smirch,
At two a forest of oak and birch,
    And then, on a platform, she:

A radiant stranger, who saw not me.
I said, 'Get out to her do I dare?'
But I kept my seat in my search for a plea,
And the wheels moved on. O could it but be
    That I had alighted there!

Nobody Comes

Tree-leaves labour up and down,
    And through them the fainting light
    Succumbs to the crawl of night.
Outside in the road the telegraph wire
    To the town from the darkening land
Intones to travellers like a spectral lyre
    Swept by a spectral hand.

A car comes up, with lamps full-glare,
    That flash upon a tree:
    It has nothing to do with me,
And whangs along in a world of its own,
    Leaving a blacker air;
And mute by the gate I stand again alone,
    And nobody pulls up there.

October 9, 1924

The Convergence of the Twain
(Lines on the loss of the 'Titanic')

I

In a solitude of the sea
Deep from human vanity,
And the Pride of Life that planned here, stilly couches
she.

II

Steel chambers, late the pyres
Of her salamandrine fires,
Cold currents thrid, and turn to rhythmic tidal lyres.

III

Over the mirrors meant
To glass the opulent
The sea-worm crawls – grotesque, slimed, dumb,
indifferent.

IV

Jewels in joy designed
To ravish the sensuous mind
Lie lightless, all their sparkles bleared and black and
blind.

V

Dim moon-eyed fishes near
Gaze at the gilded gear
And query; 'What does this vaingloriousness down
here?'

VI

Well: while was fashioning
This creature of cleaving wing,
The Immanent Will that stirs and urges everything

VII

Prepared a sinister mate
For her – so gaily great –
A Shape of Ice, for the time far and dissociate.

VIII

And as the smart ship grew
In stature, grace, and hue,
In shadowy silent distance grew the Iceberg too.

IX

Alien they seemed to be:
No mortal eye could see
The intimate welding of their later history,

X

Or sign that they were bent
By paths coincident
On being anon twin halves of one august event.

XI

Till the Spinner of the Years
Said 'Now!' And each one hears,
And consummation comes, and jars two hemispheres.

Marriage

'We Sat at the Window'
(Bournemouth, 1875)

We sat at the window looking out,
And the rain came down like silken strings
That Swithin's day. Each gutter and spout
Babbled unchecked in the busy way
    Of witless things:
Nothing to read, nothing to see
Seemed in that room for her and me
    On Swithin's day.

We were irked by the scene, by our own selves;
                                    yes,
For I did not know, nor did she infer
How much there was to read and guess
By her in me, and to see and crown
    By me in her.
Wasted were two souls in their prime,
And great was the waste, that July time
    When the rain came down.

Once at Swanage

The spray sprang up across the cusps of the moon,
    And all its light loomed green
    As a witch-flame's weirdsome sheen
At the minute of an incantation scene;
And it greened our gaze – that night at demilune.

Roaring high and roaring low was the sea
    Behind the headland shores:
    It symboled the slamming of doors,
Or a regiment hurrying over hollow floors. . . .
And there we two stood, hands clasped; I and she!

A Two-Years' Idyll

Yes; such it was;
Just those two seasons unsought,
Sweeping like summertide wind on our ways;
Moving, as straws,
Hearts quick as ours in those days;
Going like wind, too, and rated as nought
Save as the prelude to plays
Soon to come – larger, life-fraught:
Yes; such it was.

'Nought' it was called,
Even by ourselves – that which springs
Out of the years for all flesh, first or last,
Commonplace, scrawled
Dully on days that go past.
Yet, all the while, it upbore us like wings
Even in hours overcast:
Aye, though this best thing of things,
'Nought' it was called!

What seems it now?
Lost: such beginning was all;
Nothing came after: romance straight forsook
Quickly somehow
Life when we sped from our nook,
Primed for new scenes with designs smart and
tall. . . .
– A preface without any book,
A trumpet unlipped, but no call;
That seems it now.

The Musical Box

Lifelong to be
Seemed the fair colour of the time;
That there was standing shadowed near
A spirit who sang to the gentle chime
Of the self-struck notes, I did not hear,
    I did not see.

Thus did it sing
To the mindless lyre that played indoors
As she came to listen for me without:
'O value what the nonce outpours –
This best of life – that shines about
    Your welcoming!'

I had slowed along
After the torrid hours were done,
Though still the posts and walls and road
Flung back their sense of the hot-faced sun,
And had walked by Stourside Mill, where broad
    Stream-lilies throng.

And I descried
The dusky house that stood apart,
And her, white-muslined, waiting there
In the porch with high-expectant heart,
While still the thin mechanic air
    Went on inside.

At whiles would flit
Swart bats, whose wings, be-webbed and tanned,
Whirred like the wheels of ancient clocks:
She laughed a hailing as she scanned
Me in the gloom, the tuneful box
        Intoning it.

        Lifelong to be
I thought it. That there watched hard by
A spirit who sang to the indoor tune,
'O make the most of what is nigh!'
I did not hear in my dull soul-swoon –
        I did not see.

Wives in the Sere

I

Never a careworn wife but shows,
    If a joy suffuse her,
Something beautiful to those
    Patient to peruse her,
Some one charm the world unknows
    Precious to a muser,
Haply what, ere years were foes,
    Moved her mate to choose her.

II

But, be it a hint of rose
    That an instant hues her,
Or some early light or pose
    Wherewith thought renews her –
Seen by him at full, ere woes
    Practised to abuse her –
Sparely comes it, swiftly goes,
    Time again subdues her.

A Second Attempt

Thirty years after
I began again
An old-time passion:
And it seemed as fresh as when
The first day ventured on:
When mutely I would waft her
In Love's past fashion
Dreams much dwelt upon,
Dreams I wished she knew.

I went the course through,
From Love's fresh-found sensation –
Remembered still so well –
To worn words charged anew,
That left no more to tell:
Thence to hot hopes and fears,
And thence to consummation,
And thence to sober years,
Markless, and mellow-hued.

Firm the whole fabric stood,
Or seemed to stand, and sound
As it had stood before.
But nothing backward climbs,
And when I looked around
As at the former times,
There was Life – pale and hoar;
And slow it said to me,
'Twice-over cannot be!'

Love in Middle Age

He Abjures Love

At last I put off love,
    For twice ten years
The daysman of my thought,
    And hope, and doing;
Being ashamed thereof,
    And faint of fears
And desolations, wrought
    In his pursuing,

Since first in youthtime those
    Disquietings
That heart-enslavement brings
    To hale and hoary,
Became my housefellows,
    And, fool and blind,
I turned from kith and kind
    To give him glory.

I was as children be
    Who have no care;
I did not shrink or sigh,
    I did not sicken;
But lo, Love beckoned me
    And I was bare,
And poor, and starved, and dry,
    And fever-stricken.

Too many times ablaze
    With fatuous fires,
Enkindled by his wiles
    To new embraces,
Did I, by wilful ways
    And baseless ires,
Return the anxious smiles
    Of friendly faces.

No more will now rate I
    The common rare,
The midnight drizzle dew,
    The gray hour golden,
The wind a yearning cry,
    The faulty fair,
Things dreamt, of comelier hue
    Than things beholden! . . .

– I speak as one who plumbs
    Life's dim profound,
One who at length can sound
    Clear views and certain.
But – after love what comes?
    A scene that lours,
A few sad vacant hours,
    And then, the Curtain.

1883

'I Look Into My Glass'

I look into my glass,
And view my wasting skin,
And say, 'Would God it came to pass
My heart had shrunk as thin!'

For then, I, undistrest
By hearts grown cold to me,
Could lonely wait my endless rest
With equanimity.

But Time, to make me grieve,
Part steals, lets part abide;
And shakes this fragile frame at eve
With throbbings of noontide.

A Thunderstorm in Town
(A Reminiscence: 1893)

She wore a new 'terra-cotta' dress,
And we stayed, because of the pelting storm,
Within the hansom's dry recess,
Though the horse had stopped; yea, motionless
     We sat on, snug and warm.

Then the downpour ceased, to my sharp sad pain
And the glass that had screened our forms before
Flew up, and out she sprang to her door:
I should have kissed her if the rain
     Had lasted a minute more.

A Broken Appointment

You did not come,
And marching Time drew on, and wore me
                                   numb.
Yet less for loss of your dear presence there
Than that I thus found lacking in your make
That high compassion which can overbear
Reluctance for pure lovingkindness' sake
Grieved I, when, as the hope-hour stroked its
                                   sum,
You did not come.

You love not me,
And love alone can lend you loyalty;
– I know and knew it. But, unto the store
Of human deeds divine in all but name,
Was it not worth a little hour or more
To add yet this: Once you, a woman, came
To soothe a time-torn man; even though it be
You love not me?

Without, Not Within Her

It was what you bore with you, Woman,
     Not inly were,
That throned you from all else human,
     However fair!

It was that strange freshness you carried
     Into a soul
Whereon no thought of yours tarried
     Two moments at all.

And out from his spirit flew death,
     And bale, and ban,
Like the corn-chaff under the breath
     Of the winnowing-fan.

Shut out that Moon

Close up the casement, draw the blind,
　　Shut out that stealing moon,
She wears too much the guise she wore
　　Before our lutes were strewn
With years-deep dust, and names we read
　　On a white stone were hewn.

Step not forth on the dew-dashed lawn
　　To view the Lady's Chair,
Immense Orion's glittering form,
　　The Less and Greater Bear:
Stay in; to such sights we were drawn
　　When faded ones were fair.

Brush not the bough for midnight scents
　　That come forth lingeringly,
And wake the same sweet sentiments
　　They breathed to you and me
When living seemed a laugh, and love
　　All it was said to be.

Within the common lamp-lit room
　　Prison my eyes and thought;
Let dingy details crudely loom,
　　Mechanic speech be wrought:
Too fragrant was Life's early bloom,
　　Too tart the fruit it brought!

1904

After the Visit
(To F. E. D.)

Come again to the place
Where your presence was as a leaf that skims
Down a drouthy way whose ascent bedims
    The bloom on the farer's face.

Come again, with the feet
That were light on the green as a thistledown ball,
And those mute ministrations to one and to all
    Beyond a man's saying sweet.

Until then the faint scent
Of the bordering flowers swam unheeded away,
And I marked not the charm in the changes of day
    As the cloud-colours came and went.

Through the dark corridors
Your walk was so soundless I did not know
Your form from a phantom's of long ago
    Said to pass on the ancient floors,

Till you drew from the shade,
And I saw the large luminous living eyes
Regard me in fixed inquiring-wise
    As those of a soul that weighed,

Scarce consciously,
The eternal question of what Life was,
And why we were there, and by whose strange
                 laws
    That which mattered most could not be.

Remembering Emma

The Going

Why did you give no hint that night
That quickly after the morrow's dawn,
And calmly, as if indifferent quite,
You would close your term here, up and be gone
    Where I could not follow
    With wing of swallow
To gain one glimpse of you ever anon!

    Never to bid good-bye,
    Or lip me the softest call,
Or utter a wish for a word, while I
Saw morning harden upon the wall,
    Unmoved, unknowing
    That your great going
Had place that moment, and altered all.

Why do you make me leave the house
And think for a breath it is you I see
At the end of the alley of bending boughs
Where so often at dusk you used to be;
    Till in darkening dankness
    The yawning blankness
Of the perspective sickens me!

    You were she who abode
    By those red-veined rocks far West,
You were the swan-necked one who rode

Along the beetling Beeny Crest,
      And, reining nigh me,
      Would muse and eye me,
While Life unrolled us its very best.

Why, then, latterly did we not speak,
Did we not think of those days long dead,
And ere your vanishing strive to seek
That time's renewal? We might have said,
      'In this bright spring weather
      We'll visit together
Those places that once we visited.'

      Well, well! All's past amend,
      Unchangeable. It must go.
I seem but a dead man held on end
To sink down soon. . . . O you could not know
      That such swift fleeing
      No soul foreseeing –
Not even I – would undo me so!

December 1912

Your Last Drive

Here by the moorway you returned,
And saw the borough lights ahead
That lit your face – all undiscerned
To be in a week the face of the dead,
And you told of the charm of that haloed view
That never again would beam on you.

And on your left you passed the spot
Where eight days later you were to lie,
And be spoken of as one who was not;
Beholding it with a heedless eye
As alien from you, though under its tree
You soon would halt everlastingly.

I drove not with you . . . Yet had I sat
At your side that eve I should not have seen
That the countenance I was glancing at
Had a last-time look in the flickering sheen,
Nor have read the writing upon your face,
'I go hence soon to my resting-place;

'You may miss me then. But I shall not know
How many times you visit me there,
Or what your thoughts are, or if you go
There never at all. And I shall not care.
Should you censure me I shall take no heed,
And even your praises no more shall need.'

True: never you'll know. And you will not
                                        mind.
But shall I then slight you because of such?
Dear ghost, in the past did you ever find
The thought 'What profit,' move me much?
Yet abides the fact, indeed, the same, –
You are past love, praise, indifference, blame.

December 1912

The Walk

You did not walk with me
Of late to the hill-top tree
    By the gated ways,
    As in earlier days;
    You were weak and lame,
    So you never came,
And I went alone, and I did not mind,
Not thinking of you as left behind.

I walked up there to-day
Just in the former way;
    Surveyed around
    The familiar ground
    By myself again:
    What difference, then?
Only that underlying sense
Of the look of a room on returning thence.

Rain on a Grave

Clouds spout upon her
    Their waters amain
    In ruthless disdain, –
Her who but lately
    Had shivered with pain
As at touch of dishonour
If there had lit on her
So coldly, so straightly
    Such arrows of rain:

One who to shelter
    Her delicate head
Would quicken and quicken
    Each tentative tread
If drops chanced to pelt her
    That summertime spills
    In dust-paven rills
When thunder-clouds thicken
    And birds close their bills.

Would that I lay there
    And she were housed here!
Or better, together
Were folded away there
Exposed to one weather
We both, – who would stray there
When sunny the day there
    Or evening was clear
    At the prime of the year.

Soon will be growing
   Green blades from her mound,
And daisies be showing
   Like stars on the ground,
Till she form part of them –
Ay – the sweet heart of them,
Loved beyond measure
With a child's pleasure
   All her life's round.

   Jan. 31, 1913

'I Found Her Out There'

I found her out there
On a slope few see,
That falls westwardly
To the salt-edged air,
Where the ocean breaks
On the purple strand,
And the hurricane shakes
The solid land.

I brought her here,
And have laid her to rest
In a noiseless nest
No sea beats near.
She will never be stirred
In her loamy cell
By the waves long heard
And loved so well.

So she does not sleep
By those haunted heights
The Atlantic smites
And the blind gales sweep,
Whence she often would gaze
At Dundagel's famed head,
While the dipping blaze
Dyed her face fire-red;

And would sigh at the tale
Of sunk Lyonnesse,
As a wind-tugged tress

Flapped her cheek like a flail;
Or listen at whiles
With a thought-bound brow
To the murmuring miles
She is far from now.

Yet her shade, maybe,
Will creep underground
Till it catch the sound
Of that western sea
As it swells and sobs
Where she once domiciled,
And joy in its throbs
With the heart of a child.

Without Ceremony

It was your way, my dear,
To vanish without a word
When callers, friends, or kin
Had left, and I hastened in
To rejoin you, as I inferred.

And when you'd a mind to career
Off anywhere – say to town –
You were all on a sudden gone
Before I had thought thereon,
Or noticed your trunks were down.

So, now that you disappear
For ever in that swift style,
Your meaning seems to me
Just as it used to be:
'Good-bye is not worth while!'

Lament

How she would have loved
A party to-day! –
Bright-hatted and gloved,
With table and tray
And chairs on the lawn
Her smiles would have shone
With welcomings. . . . But
She is shut, she is shut
    From friendship's spell
    In the jailing shell
    Of her tiny cell.

Or she would have reigned
At a dinner to-night
With ardours unfeigned,
And a generous delight;
All in her abode
She'd have freely bestowed
On her guests. . . . But alas,
She is shut under grass
    Where no cups flow,
    Powerless to know
    That it might be so.

And she would have sought
With a child's eager glance
The shy snowdrops brought
By the new year's advance,
And peered in the rime
Of Candlemas-time

For crocuses . . . chanced
It that she were not tranced
    From sights she loved best;
    Wholly possessed
    By an infinite rest!

And we are here staying
Amid these stale things,
Who care not for gaying,
And those junketings
That used so to joy her,
And never to cloy her
As us they cloy! . . . But
She is shut, she is shut
    From the cheer of them, dead
    To all done and said
    In her yew-arched bed.

The Haunter

He does not think that I haunt here nightly:
    How shall I let him know
That whither his fancy sets him wandering
    I, too, alertly go? –
Hover and hover a few feet from him
    Just as I used to do,
But cannot answer the words he lifts me –
    Only listen thereto!

When I could answer he did not say them
    When I could let him know
How I would like to join in his journeys
    Seldom he wished to go.
Now that he goes and wants me with him
    More than he used to do,
Never he sees my faithful phantom
    Though he speaks thereto.

Yes, I companion him to places
    Only dreamers know,
Where the shy hares print long paces,
    Where the night rooks go;
Into old aisles where the past is all to him,
    Close as his shade can do,
Always lacking the power to call to him,
    Near as I reach thereto!

What a good haunter I am, O tell him!
    Quickly make him know
If he but sigh since my loss befell him
    Straight to his side I go.
Tell him a faithful one is doing
    All that love can do
Still that his path may be worth pursuing,
    And to bring peace thereto.

The Voice

Woman much missed, how you call to me, call to me,
Saying that now you are not as you were
When you had changed from the one who was all to me,
But as at first, when our day was fair.

Can it be you that I hear? Let me view you, then,
Standing as when I drew near to the town
Where you would wait for me: yes, as I knew you then,
Even to the original air-blue gown!

Or is it only the breeze, in its listlessness
Travelling across the wet mead to me here,
You being ever dissolved to wan wistlessness,
Heard no more again far or near?

    Thus I; faltering forward,
    Leaves around me falling,
Wind oozing thin through the thorn from norward,
    And the woman calling.

December 1912

A Dream or No

Why go to Saint-Juliot? What's Juliot to me?
           Some strange necromancy
           But charmed me to fancy
That much of my life claims the spot as its key.

Yes. I have had dreams of that place in the West,
           And a maiden abiding
           Thereat as in hiding;
Fair-eyed and white-shouldered, broad-browed and
                             brown-tressed.

And of how, coastward bound on a night long ago,
           There lonely I found her,
           The sea-birds around her,
And other than nigh things uncaring to know.

So sweet her life there (in my thought has it
                      seemed)
           That quickly she drew me
           To take her unto me,
And lodge her long years with me. Such have I
                      dreamed.

But nought of that maid from Saint-Juliot I see;
           Can she ever have been here,
           And shed her life's sheen here,
The woman I thought a long housemate with me?

Does there even a place like Saint-Juliot exist?
Or a Valency Valley
With stream and leafed alley,
Or Beeny, or Bos with its flounce flinging mist?

February 1913

After a Journey

Hereto I come to view a voiceless ghost;
    Whither, O whither will its whim now draw me?
Up the cliff, down, till I'm lonely, lost,
    And the unseen waters' ejaculations awe me.
Where you will next be there's no knowing,
    Facing round about me everywhere,
        With your nut-coloured hair,
And gray eyes, and rose-flush coming and going.

Yes: I have re-entered your olden haunts at last;
    Through the years, through the dead scenes I have
        tracked you;
What have you now found to say of our past –
    Scanned across the dark space wherein I have lacked
                                                    you?
Summer gave us sweets, but autumn wrought division?
    Things were not lastly as firstly well
        With us twain, you tell?
But all's closed now, despite Time's derision.

I see what you are doing: you are leading me on
    To the spots we knew when we haunted here together,
The waterfall, above which the mist-bow shone
    At the then fair hour in the then fair weather,
And the cave just under, with a voice still so hollow
    That it seems to call out to me from forty years ago,
        When you were all aglow,
And not the thin ghost that I now fraily follow!

Ignorant of what there is flitting here to see,
   The waked birds preen and the seals flop lazily;
Soon you will have, Dear, to vanish from me,
   For the stars close their shutters and the dawn whitens
                                                    hazily.
Trust me, I mind not, though Life lours,
   The bringing me here; nay, bring me here again!
      I am just the same as when
Our days were a joy, and our paths through flowers.

   Pentargan Bay

Beeny Cliff
March 1870–March 1913

I

O the opal and the sapphire of that wandering western
                                                    sea,
And the woman riding high above with bright hair
                                        flapping free –
The woman whom I loved so, and who loyally loved me.

II

The pale mews plained below us, and the waves seemed
                                            far away
In a nether sky, engrossed in saying their ceaseless
                                        babbling say,
As we laughed light-heartedly aloft on that clear-sunned
                                            March day.

III

A little cloud then cloaked us, and there flew an irised
                                            rain,
And the Atlantic dyed its levels with a dull misfeatured
                                            stain,
And then the sun burst out again, and purples prinked
                                        the main.

IV

– Still in all its chasmal beauty bulks old Beeny to the
                                            sky,
And shall she and I not go there once again now March
                                        is nigh,
And the sweet things said in that March say anew there
                                        by and by?

What is still in chasmal beauty looms that wild weird
                                        western shore,
The woman now is – elsewhere – whom the ambling
                                        pony bore,
And nor knows nor cares for Beeny, and will laugh there
                                        nevermore.

At Castle Boterel

As I drive to the junction of lane and highway,
   And the drizzle bedrenches the waggonette,
I look behind at the fading byway,
   And see on its slope, now glistening wet,
      Distinctly yet

Myself and a girlish form benighted
   In dry March weather. We climb the road
Beside a chaise. We had just alighted
   To ease the sturdy pony's load
      When he sighed and slowed.

What we did as we climbed, and what we talked of
   Matters not much, nor to what it led, –
Something that life will not be balked of
   Without rude reason till hope is dead,
      And feeling fled.

It filled but a minute. But was there ever
   A time of such quality, since or before,
In that hill's story? To one mind never,
   Though it has been climbed, foot-swift,
               foot-sore,
      By thousands more.

Primaeval rocks form the road's steep border,
   And much have they faced there, first and last,
Of the transitory in Earth's long order;
   But what they record in colour and cast
      Is – that we two passed.

And to me, though Time's unflinching rigour,
    In mindless rote, has ruled from sight
The substance now, one phantom figure
    Remains on the slope, as when that night
        Saw us alight.

I look and see it there, shrinking, shrinking,
    I look back at it amid the rain
For the very last time; for my sand is sinking,
    And I shall traverse old love's domain
        Never again.

March 1913

The Phantom Horsewoman

I

Queer are the ways of a man I know:
  He comes and stands
  In a careworn craze,
  And looks at the sands
  And the seaward haze
  With moveless hands
  And face and gaze,
  Then turns to go . . .
And what does he see when he gazes so?

II

They say he sees as an instant thing
  More clear than to-day,
  A sweet soft scene
  That was once in play
  By that briny green;
  Yes, notes alway
  Warm, real, and keen,
  What his back years bring –
A phantom of his own figuring.

Of this vision of his they might say more:
      Not only there
      Does he see this sight,
      But everywhere
      In his brain – day, night,
      As if on the air
      It were drawn rose-bright –
      Yea, far from that shore
Does he carry this vision of heretofore:

        IV

A ghost-girl-rider. And though, toil-tried,
      He withers daily,
      Time touches her not,
      But she still rides gaily
      In his rapt thought
      On that shagged and shaly
      Atlantic spot,
      And as when first eyed
Draws rein and sings to the swing of the tide.

1913

More about Emma

Under the Waterfall

'Whenever I plunge my arm, like this,
In a basin of water, I never miss
The sweet sharp sense of a fugitive day
Fetched back from its thickening shroud of gray.
        Hence the only prime
        And real love-rhyme
        That I know by heart,
        And that leaves no smart,
Is the purl of a little valley fall
About three spans wide and two spans tall
Over a table of solid rock,
And into a scoop of the self-same block;
The purl of a runlet that never ceases
In stir of kingdoms, in wars, in peaces;
With a hollow boiling voice it speaks
And has spoken since hills were turfless peaks.'

'And why gives this the only prime
Idea to you of a real love-rhyme?
And why does plunging your arm in a bowl
Full of spring water, bring throbs to your soul?'

'Well, under the fall, in a crease of the stone,
Though where precisely none ever has known,
Jammed darkly, nothing to show how prized,
And by now with its smoothness opalized,
        Is a drinking-glass:
        For, down that pass
        My lover and I
        Walked under a sky

Of blue with a leaf-wove awning of green,
In the burn of August, to paint the scene,
And we placed our basket of fruit and wine
By the runlet's rim, where we sat to dine;
And when we had drunk from the glass together,
Arched by the oak-copse from the weather,
I held the vessel to rinse in the fall,
Where it slipped, and sank, and was past recall,
Though we stooped and plumbed the little abyss
With long bared arms. There the glass still is.
And, as said, if I thrust my arm below
Cold water in basin or bowl, a throe
From the past awakens a sense of that time,
And the glass we used, and the cascade's rhyme.
The basin seems the pool, and its edge
The hard smooth face of the brook-side ledge,
And the leafy pattern of china-ware
The hanging plants that were bathing there.

'By night, by day, when it shines our lours,
There lies intact that chalice of ours,
And its presence adds to the rhyme of love
Persistently sung by the fall above.
No lip has touched it since his and mine
In turns therefrom sipped lovers' wine.'

When Oats Were Reaped

That day when oats were reaped, and wheat was ripe,
 and barley ripening,
  The road-dust hot, and the bleaching grasses dry,
   I walked along and said,
While looking just ahead to where some silent people lie:

'I wounded one who's there, and now know well I
 wounded her;
  But, ah, she does not know that she wounded me!'
   And not an air stirred,
Nor a bill of any bird; and no response accorded she.

August 1913

'She Opened the Door'

She opened the door of the West to me,
    With its loud sea-lashings,
    And cliff-side clashings
Of waters rife with revelry.

She opened the door of Romance to me,
    The door from a cell
    I had known too well,
Too long, till then, and was fain to flee.

She opened the door of a Love to me,
    That passed the wry
    World-welters by
As far as the arching blue the lea.

She opens the door of the Past to me,
    Its magic lights,
    Its heavenly heights,
When forward little is to see!

1913

At the word 'Farewell'

She looked like a bird from a cloud
    On the clammy lawn,
Moving alone, bare-browed
    In the dim of dawn.
The candles alight in the room
    For my parting meal
Made all things withoutdoors loom
    Strange, ghostly, unreal.

The hour itself was a ghost,
    And it seemed to me then
As of chances the chance furthermost
    I should see her again.
I beheld not where all was so fleet
    That a Plan of the past
Which had ruled us from birthtime to meet
    Was in working at last:

No prelude did I there perceive
    To a drama at all,
Or foreshadow what fortune might weave
    From beginnings so small;
But I rose as if quicked by a spur
    I was bound to obey,
And stepped through the casement to her
    Still alone in the gray.

'I am leaving you. . . . Farewell!' I said
    As I followed her on
By an alley bare boughs overspread;
    'I soon must be gone!'
Even then the scale might have been turned
    Against love by a feather,
– But crimson one cheek of hers burned
    When we came in together.

The Frozen Greenhouse
(St. Juliot)

'There was a frost
Last night!' she said,
'And the stove was forgot
When we went to bed,
And the greenhouse plants
Are frozen dead!'

By the breakfast blaze
Blank-faced spoke she,
Her scared young look
Seeming to be
The very symbol
Of tragedy.

The frost is fiercer
Than then to-day,
As I pass the place
Of her once dismay,
But the greenhouse stands
Warm, tight, and gay,

While she who grieved
At the sad lot
Of her pretty plants –
Cold, iced, forgot –
Herself is colder,
And knows it not.

Days to Recollect

Do you recall
That day in Fall
When we walked towards Saint Alban's Head,
On thistledown that summer had shed,
Or must I remind you?
Winged thistle-seeds which hitherto
Had lain as none were there, or few,
But rose at the brush of your petticoat-seam
(As ghosts might rise of the recent dead),
And sailed on the breeze in a nebulous stream
Like a comet's tail behind you:
You don't recall
That day in Fall?

Then do you remember
That sad November
When you left me never to see me more,
And looked quite other than theretofore,
As if it could not *be* you?
And lay by the window whence you had gazed
So many times when blamed or praised,
Morning or noon, through years and years,
Accepting the gifts that Fortune bore,
Sharing, enduring, joys, hopes, fears!
Well: I never more did see you. –
Say you remember
That sad November!

'Something Tapped'

Something tapped on the pane of my room
    When there was never a trace
Of wind or rain, and I saw in the gloom
    My weary Belovéd's face.

'O I am tired of waiting,' she said,
    'Night, morn, noon, afternoon;
So cold it is in my lonely bed,
    And I thought you would join me soon!'

I rose and neared the window-glass,
    But vanished thence had she:
Only a pallid moth, alas,
    Tapped at the pane for me.

August 1913

The Peace Offering

It was but a little thing,
Yet I knew it meant to me
Ease from what had given a sting
To the very birdsinging
    Latterly.

But I would not welcome it;
And for all I then declined
O the regrettings infinite
When the night-processions flit
    Through the mind!

He Prefers her Earthly

This after-sunset is a sight for seeing,
Cliff-heads of craggy cloud surrounding it.
 – And dwell you in that glory-show?
You may; for there are strange strange things in
                                           being,
      Stranger than I know.

Yet if that chasm of splendour claim your presence
Which glows between the ash cloud and the dun,
   How changed must be your mortal mould!
Changed to a firmament-riding earthless essence
      From what you were of old:

All too unlike the fond and fragile creature
Then known to me. . . . Well, shall I say it plain?
   I would not have you thus and there,
But still would grieve on, missing you, still feature
      You as the one you were.

The West-of-Wessex Girl

A very West-of-Wessex girl,
   As blithe as blithe could be,
   Was once well-known to me,
And she would laud her native town,
   And hope and hope that we
Might sometime study up and down
   Its charms in company.

But never I squired my Wessex girl
   In jaunts to Hoe or street
   When hearts were high in beat,
Nor saw her in the marbled ways
   Where market-people meet
That in her bounding early days
   Were friendly with her feet.

Yet now my West-of-Wessex girl,
   When midnight hammers slow
   From Andrew's, blow by blow,
As phantom draws me by the hand
   To the place – Plymouth Hoe –
Where side by side in life, as planned,
   We never were to go!

Begun in Plymouth, March 1913

The Little Old Table

Creak, little wood thing, creak,
When I touch you with elbow or knee;
That is the way you speak
Of one who gave you to me!

You, little table, she brought –
Brought me with her own hand,
As she looked at me with a thought
That I did not understand.

– Whoever owns it anon,
And hears it, will never know
What a history hangs upon
This creak from long ago.

On a Discovered Curl of Hair

When your soft welcomings were said,
This curl was waving on your head,
And when we walked where breakers dinned
It sported in the sun and wind,
And when I had won your words of grace
It brushed and clung about my face.
Then, to abate the misery
Of absentness, you gave it me.

Where are its fellows now? Ah, they
For brightest brown have donned a gray,
And gone into a caverned ark,
Ever unopened, always dark!

Yet this one curl, untouched of time,
Beams with live brown as in its prime,
So that it seems I even could now
Restore it to the living brow
By bearing down the western road
Till I had reached your old abode.

February 1913

Two Lips

I kissed them in fancy as I came
　　　Away in the morning glow:
I kissed them through the glass of her picture-frame:
　　　She did not know.

I kissed them in love, in troth, in laughter,
　　　When she knew all; long so!
That I should kiss them in a shroud thereafter
　　　She did not know.

The Tresses

'When the air was damp
It made my curls hang slack
As they kissed my neck and back
While I footed the salt-aired track
    I loved to tramp.

'When it was dry
They would roll up crisp and tight
As I went on in the light
Of the sun, which my own sprite
    Seemed to outvie.

'Now I am old;
And have not one gay curl
As I had when a girl
For dampness to unfurl
    Or sun uphold!'

The Last Performance

'I am playing my oldest tunes,' declared she,
    'All the old tunes I know, –
Those I learnt ever so long ago.'
– Why she should think just then she'd play them
    Silence cloaks like snow.

When I returned from the town at nightfall
    Notes continued to pour
As when I had left two hours before:
'It's the very last time,' she said in closing;
    'From now I play no more.'

A few morns onward found her fading,
    And, as her life outflew,
I thought of her playing her tunes right through;
And I felt she had known of what was coming,
    And wondered how she knew.

1912

'If you Had Known'

If you had known
When listening with her to the far-down moan
Of the white-selvaged and empurpled sea,
And rain came on that did not hinder talk,
Or damp your flashing facile gaiety
In turning home, despite the slow wet walk
By crooked ways, and over stiles of stone;
If you had known

You would lay roses,
Fifty years thence, on her monument, that
discloses
Its graying shape upon the luxuriant green;
Fifty years thence to an hour, by chance led there,
What might have moved you? – yea, had you
foreseen
That on the tomb of the selfsame one, gone
where
The dawn of every day is as the close is,
You would lay roses!

1920

War

The Dead Drummer

I

They throw in Drummer Hodge, to rest
    Uncoffined – just as found:
His landmark is a kopje-crest
    That breaks the veldt around;
And foreign constellations west
    Each night above his mound.

II

Young Hodge the Drummer never knew –
    Fresh from his Wessex home –
The meaning of the broad Karoo,
    The Bush, the dusty loam,
And why uprose to nightly view
    Strange stars amid the gloam.

III

Yet portion of that unknown plain
    Will Hodge for ever be;
His homely Northern breast and brain
    Grow to some Southern tree,
And strange-eyed constellations reign
    His stars eternally.

Channel Firing

That night your great guns, unawares,
Shook all our coffins as we lay,
And broke the chancel window-squares,
We thought it was the Judgment-day

And sat upright. While drearisome
Arose the howl of wakened hounds:
The mouse let fall the altar-crumb,
The worms drew back into the mounds,

The glebe cow drooled. Till God called, 'No:
It's gunnery practice out at sea
Just as before you went below;
The world is as it used to be:

'All nations striving strong to make
Red war yet redder. Mad as hatters
They do no more for Christés sake
Than you who are helpless in such matters.

'That this is not the judgment-hour
For some of them's a blessed thing,
For if it were they'd have to scour
Hell's floor for so much threatening. . . .

'Ha, ha. It will be warmer when
I blow the trumpet (if indeed
I ever do; for you are men,
And rest eternal sorely need).'

So down we lay again. 'I wonder,
Will the world ever saner be,'
Said one, 'than when He sent us under
In our indifferent century!'

And many a skeleton shook his head.
'Instead of preaching forty year,'
My neighbour Parson Thirdly said,
'I wish I had stuck to pipes and beer.'

Again the guns disturbed the hour,
Roaring their readiness to avenge,
As far inland as Stourton Tower,
And Camelot, and starlit Stonehenge.

April 1914

The Pity of It

I walked in loamy Wessex lanes, afar
From rail-track and from highway, and I heard
In field and farmstead many an ancient word
Of local lineage like 'Thu bist,' 'Er war,'

'Ich woll,' 'Er sholl,' and by-talk similar,
Nigh as they speak who in this month's moon gird
At England's very loins, thereunto spurred
By gangs whose glory threats and slaughters are.

Then seemed a Heart crying: 'Whosoever they be
At root and bottom of this, who flung this flame
Between kin folk kin tongued even as are we,

'Sinister, ugly, lurid, be their fame;
May their familiars grow to shun their name,
And their brood perish everlastingly.'

April 1915

Chorus of the Years
(from *The Dynasts* – Hardy is describing
the field of Waterloo before the battle)

Yea, the coneys are scared by the thud of hoofs,
And their white scuts flash at their vanishing
                                  heels,
And swallows abandon the hamlet-roofs.

The mole's tunnelled chambers are crushed by
                                  wheels,
The lark's eggs scattered, their owners fled;
And the hedgehog's household the sapper unseals.

The snail draws in at the terrible tread,
But in vain; he is crushed by the felloe-rim;
The worm asks what can be overhead,

And wriggles deep from a scene so grim,
And guesses him safe; for he does not know
What a foul red flood will be soaking him!

Beaten about by the heel and toe
Are butterflies, sick of the day's long rheum,
To die of a worse than the weather-foe.

Trodden and bruised to a miry tomb
Are ears that have greened but will never be gold,
And flowers in the bud that will never bloom.

In Time of 'The Breaking of Nations'

I

Only a man harrowing clods
    In a slow silent walk
With an old horse that stumbles and nods
    Half asleep as they stalk.

II

Only thin smoke without flame
    From the heaps of couch-grass;
Yet this will go onward the same
    Though Dynasties pass.

III

Yonder a maid and her wight
    Come whispering by:
War's annals will cloud into night
    Ere their story die.

1915

On Himself

On a Midsummer Eve

I idly cut a parsley stalk,
And blew therein towards the moon;
I had not thought what ghosts would walk
With shivering footsteps to my tune.

I went, and knelt, and scooped my hand
As if to drink, into the brook,
And a faint figure seemed to stand
Above me, with the bygone look.

I lipped rough rhymes of chance, not choice,
I thought not what my words might be;
There came into my ear a voice
That turned a tenderer verse for me.

Wessex Heights
(1896)

There are some heights in Wessex, shaped as if by a
                          kindly hand
For thinking, dreaming, dying on, and at crises when I
                          stand,
Say, on Ingpen Beacon eastward, or on Wylls-Neck
                          westwardly,
I seem where I was before my birth, and after death may
                          be.

In the lowlands I have no comrade, not even the lone
                          man's friend –
Her who suffereth long and is kind; accepts what he is
                          too weak to mend:
Down there they are dubious and askance; there nobody
                          thinks as I,
But mind-chains do not clank where one's next
                    neighbour is the sky.

In the towns I am tracked by phantoms having weird
                          detective ways –
Shadows of beings who fellowed with myself of earlier
                          days:
They hang about at places, and they say harsh heavy
                          things –
Men with a wintry sneer, and women with tart
                    disparagings.

Down there I seem to be false to myself, my simple self
                          that was,

And is not now, and I see him watching, wondering
                              what crass cause
Can have merged him into such a strange continuator as
                                             this,
Who yet has something in common with himself, my
                                     chrysalis.

I cannot go to the great grey Plain; there's a figure
                              against the moon,
Nobody sees it but I, and it makes my breast beat out of
                                            tune;
I cannot go to the tall-spired town, being barred by the
                                  forms now passed
For everybody but me, in whose long vision they stand
                                        there fast.

There's a ghost at Yell'ham Bottom chiding loud at the
                                 fall of the night,
There's a ghost in Froom-side Vale, thin-lipped and
                          vague, in a shroud of white,
There is one in the railway train whenever I do not want
                                          it near,
I see its profile against the pane, saying what I would not
                                           hear.

As for one rare fair woman, I am now but a thought of
                                           hers,
I enter her mind and another thought succeeds me that
                                      she prefers;
Yet my love for her in its fulness she herself even did not
                                          know;
Well, time cures hearts of tenderness, and now I can let
                                       her go.

So I am found on Ingpen Beacon, or on Wylls-Neck to
                                        the west,
Or else on homely Bulbarrow, or little Pilsdon Crest,
Where men have never cared to haunt, nor woman have
                                        walked with me,
And ghosts then keep their distance; and I know some
                                        liberty.

Lines
To a Movement in Mozart's E-Flat Symphony

Show me again the time
When in the Junetide's prime
We flew by meads and mountains northerly! –
Yea, to such freshness, fairness, fulness, fineness,
freeness,
    Love lures life on.

Show me again the day
When from the sandy bay
We looked together upon the pestered sea! –
Yea, to such surging, swaying, sighing, swelling,
shrinking,
    Loves lures life on.

Show me again the hour
When by the pinnacled tower
We eyed each other and feared futurity! –
Yea, to such bodings, broodings, beatings,
blanchings, blessings,
    Love lures life on.

Show me again just this:
The moment of that kiss
Away from the prancing folk, by the
strawberry-tree! –
Yea, to such rashness, ratheness, rareness, ripeness,
richness,
    Love lures life on.

Begun November 1898

Self-Unconscious

Along the way
He walked that day,
Watching shapes that reveries limn,
And seldom he
Had eyes to see
The moment that encompassed him.

Bright yellowhammers
Made mirthful clamours,
And billed long straws with a bustling air,
And bearing their load
Flew up the road
That he followed, alone, without interest there.

From bank to ground
And over and round
They sidled along the adjoining hedge;
Sometimes to the gutter
Their yellow flutter
Would dip from the nearest slatestone ledge.

The smooth sea-line
With a metal shine,
And flashes of white, and a sail thereon,
He would also descry
With a half-wrapt eye
Between the projects he mused upon.

Yes, round him were these
Earth's artistries,
But specious plans that came to his call
Did most engage
His pilgrimage,
While himself he did not see at all.

Dead now as sherds
Are the yellow birds,
And all that mattered has passed away;
Yet God, the Elf,
Now shows him that self
As he was, and should have been shown, that day.

O it would have been good
Could he then have stood
At a clear-eyed distance, and conned the whole,
But now such vision
Is mere derision,
Nor soothes his body nor saves his soul.

Not much, some may
Incline to say,
To see therein, had it all been seen.
Nay! he is aware
A thing was there
That loomed with an immortal mien.

Near Bossiney

Penance

'Why do you sit, O pale thin man,
        At the end of the room
By that harpsichord, built on the quaint old
                                plan?
        – It is cold as a tomb,
And there's not a spark within the grate;
        And the jingling wires
        Are as vain desires
        That have lagged too late.'

'Why do I? Alas, far times ago
        A woman lyred here
In the evenfall; one who fain did so
        From year to year;
And, in loneliness bending wistfully,
        Would wake each note
        In sick sad rote,
        None to listen or see!

'I would not join. I would not stay,
        But drew away,
Though the winter fire beamed brightly. . .
                                Aye!
        I do to-day
What I would not then; and the chill old keys,
        Like a skull's brown teeth
        Loose in their sheath,
        Freeze my touch; yes, freeze.'

Surview

'Cogitavi vias meas'

A cry from the green-grained sticks of the fire
    Made me gaze where it seemed to be:
'Twas my own voice talking therefrom to me
On how I had walked when my sun was higher –
    My heart in its arrogancy.

'You held not to whatsoever was true,'
    Said my own voice talking to me:
'Whatsoever was just you were slack to see;
Kept not things lovely and pure in view,'
    Said my own voice talking to me.

'You slighted her that endureth all,'
    Said my own voice talking to me;
'Vaunteth not, trusteth hopefully;
That suffereth long and is kind withal,'
    Said my own voice talking to me.

'You taught not that which you set about,'
    Said my own voice talking to me;
'That the greatest of things is Charity. . . .'
– And the sticks burnt low, and the fire went out,
    And my voice ceased talking to me.

Afterwards

When the Present has latched its postern behind my
tremulous stay,
And the May month flaps its glad green leaves like
wings,
Delicate-filmed as new-spun silk, will the neighbours
say,
'He was a man who used to notice such things'?

If it be in the dusk when, like an eyelid's soundless blink,
The dewfall-hawk comes crossing the shades to alight
Upon the wind-warped upland thorn, a gazer may think,
'To him this must have been a familiar sight.'

If I pass during some nocturnal blackness, mothy and
warm,
When the hedgehog travels furtively over the lawn,
One may say, 'He strove that such innocent creatures
should come to no harm,
But he could do little for them; and now he is gone.'

If, when hearing that I have been stilled at last, they
stand at the door,
Watching the full-starred heavens that winter sees,
Will this thought rise on those who will meet my face no
more,
'He was one who had an eye for such mysteries'?

And will any say when my bell of quittance is heard in
                         the gloom
  And a crossing breeze cuts a pause in its outrollings,
Till they rise again, as they were a new bell's boom,
  'He hears it not now, but used to notice such things'?

So Various

You may have met a man – quite young –
A brisk-eyed youth, and highly strung:
    One whose desires
    And inner fires
    Moved him as wires.

And you may have met one stiff and old,
If not in years; of manner cold;
    Who seemed as stone,
    And never had known
    Of mirth or moan.

And there may have crossed your path a lover,
In whose clear depths you could discover
    A staunch, robust,
    And tender trust,
    Through storm and gust.

And you may have also known one fickle,
Whose fancies changed as the silver sickle
    Of yonder moon,
    Which shapes so soon
    To demilune!

You entertained a person once
Whom you internally deemed a dunce: –
    As he sat in view
    Just facing you
    You saw him through.

You came to know a learned seer
Of whom you read the surface mere:
        Your soul quite sank;
        Brain of such rank
        Dubbed yours a blank.

Anon you quizzed a man of sadness,
Who never could have known true gladness:
        Just for a whim
        You pitied him
        In his sore trim.

You journeyed with a man so glad
You never could conceive him sad:
        He proved to be
        Indubitably
        Good company.

You lit on an unadventurous slow man,
Who, said you, need be feared by no man;
        That his slack deeds
        And sloth must needs
        Produce but weeds.

A man of enterprise, shrewd and swift,
Who never suffered affairs to drift,
        You eyed for a time
        Just in his prime
        And judged he might climb.

You smoked beside one who forgot
All that you said, or grasped it not.
    Quite a poor thing,
    Not worth a sting
    By satirizing!

Next year you nearly lost for ever
Goodwill from one who forgot slights never;
    And, with unease,
    Felt you must seize
    Occasion to please . . .

Now. . . . All these specimens of man,
So various in their pith and plan,
    Curious to say
    Were *one* man. Yea,
    I was all they.

Moments of Vision

That mirror
Which makes of men a transparency,
    Who holds that mirror
And bids us such a breast-bare spectacle see
    Of you and me?

That mirror
Whose magic penetrates like a dart,
    Who lifts that mirror
And throws our mind back on us, and our heart,
    Until we start?

That mirror
Works well in these night hours of ache;
    Why in that mirror
Are tincts we never see ourselves once take
    When the world is awake?

That mirror
Can test each mortal when unaware;
    Yea, that strange mirror
May catch his last thoughts, whole life foul or
                                    fair,
    Glassing it – where?

'Who's in the Next Room?'

'Who's in the next room? – who?
          I seemed to see
Somebody in the dawning passing through,
          Unknown to me.'
'Nay: you saw nought. He passed invisibly.'

'Who's in the next room? – who?
          I seem to hear
Somebody muttering firm in a language new
          That chills the ear.'
'No: you catch not his tongue who has entered
                              there.'

'Who's in the next room? – who?
          I seem to feel
His breath like a clammy draught, as if it drew
          From the Polar Wheel.'
'No: none who breathes at all does the door
                              conceal.'

'Who's in the next room? – who?
          A figure wan
With a message to one in there of something due?
          Shall I know him anon?'
'Yea he; and he brought such; and you'll know him
                              anon.'

Lying Awake

You, Morningtide Star, now are steady-eyed, over the
                                                     east,
    I know it as if I saw you;
You, Beeches, engrave on the sky your thin twigs, even
                                                    the least;
    Had I paper and pencil I'd draw you.

You, Meadow, are white with your counterpane cover
                                                   of dew,
    I see it as if I were there;
You, Churchyard, are lightening faint from the shade of
                                                   the yew.
    The names creeping out everywhere.

When Dead
To ——

It will be much better when
    I am under the bough;
I shall be more myself, Dear, then,
    Than I am now.

No sign of querulousness
    To wear you out
Shall I show there: strivings and stress
    Be quite without.

This fleeting life-brief blight
    Will have gone past
When I resume my old and right
    Place in the Vast.

And when you come to me
    To show you true,
Doubt not I shall infallibly
    Be waiting you.

'Regret Not Me'

Regret not me;
Beneath the sunny tree
I lie uncaring, slumbering peacefully.

Swift as the light
I flew my faery flight;
Ecstatically I moved, and feared no night.

I did not know
That heydays fade and go,
But deemed that what was would be always so.

I skipped at morn
Between the yellowing corn,
Thinking it good and glorious to be born.

I ran at eves
Among the piled-up sheaves,
Dreaming, 'I grieve not, therefore nothing
grieves.'

Now soon will come
The apple, pear, and plum,
And hinds will sing, and autumn insects hum.

Again you will fare
To cider-makings rare,
And junketings; but I shall not be there.

Yet gaily sing
Until the pewter ring
Those songs we sang when we went gipsying.

And lightly dance
Some triple-timed romance
In coupled figures, and forget mischance;

And mourn not me
Beneath the yellowing tree;
For I shall mind not, slumbering peacefully.

People and Stories

The Schreckhorn
(With thoughts of Leslie Stephen)
(June 1897)

Aloof, as if a thing of mood and whim;
Now that its spare and desolate figure gleams
Upon my nearing vision, less it seems
A looming Alp-height than a guise of him
Who scaled its horn with ventured life and limb,
Drawn on by vague imaginings, maybe,
Of semblance to his personality
In its quaint glooms, keen lights, and rugged trim.
At his last change, when Life's dull coils unwind,
Will he, in old love, hitherward escape,
And the eternal essence of his mind
Enter this silent adamantine shape,
And his low voicing haunt its slipping snows
When dawn that calls the climber dyes them rose?

At Lulworth Cove a Century Back

Had I but lived a hundred years ago
I might have gone, as I have gone this year,
By Warmwell Cross on to a Cove I know,
And Time have placed his finger on me there:

'You see that man?' – I might have looked, and
                                    said,
'Oh yes: I see him. One that boat has brought
Which dropped down Channel round Saint Alban's
                                    Head.
So commonplace a youth calls not my thought.'

'You see that man?' – 'Why yes; I told you; yes:
Of an idling town-sort; thin; hair brown in hue;
And as the evening light scants less and less
He looks up at a star, as many do.'

'You see that man?' – 'Nay, leave me!' then I plead,
'I have fifteen miles to vamp across the lea,
And it grows dark, and I am weary-kneed:
I have said the third time; yes, that man I see!'

'Good. That man goes to Rome – to death, despair;
And no one notes him now but you and I:
A hundred years, and the world will follow him
                                    there,
And bend with reverence where his ashes lie.'

September 1920

Note. – In September 1820 Keats, on his way to Rome, landed one day on the Dorset coast, and composed the sonnet, 'Bright star! would I were steadfast as thou art.' The spot of his landing is judged to have been Lulworth Cove.

During Wind and Rain

They sing their dearest songs –
He, she, all of them – yea,
Treble and tenor and bass,
    And one to play;
With the candles mooning each face. . . .
    Ah, no; the years O!
How the sick leaves reel down in throngs!

They clear the creeping moss –
Elders and juniors – aye,
Making the pathways neat
    And the garden gay;
And they build a shady seat. . . .
    Ah, no; the years, the years;
See, the white storm-birds wing across!

They are blithely breakfasting all –
Men and maidens – yea,
Under the summer tree,
    With a glimpse of the bay,
While pet fowl come to the knee. . . .
    Ah, no; the years O!
And the rotten rose is ript from the wall.

They change to a high new house,
He, she, all of them – aye,
Clocks and carpets and chairs
   On the lawn all day,
And brightest things that are theirs. . . .
   Ah, no; the years, the years;
Down their carved names the rain-drop
                              ploughs.

The Lodging-House Fuchsias

Mrs Masters's fuchsias hung
Higher and broader, and brightly swung,
    Bell-like, more and more
Over the narrow garden-path,
Giving the passer a sprinkle-bath
       In the morning.

She put up with their pushful ways,
And made us tenderly lift their sprays,
    Going to her door:
But when her funeral had to pass
They cut back all the flowery mass
       In the morning.

In a London Flat

I

'You look like a widower,' she said
Through the folding-doors with a laugh from the bed,
As he sat by the fire in the outer room,
Reading late on a night of gloom,
And a cab-hack's wheeze, and the clap of its feet
In its breathless pace on the smooth wet street,
Were all that came to them now and then. . . .
'You really do!' she quizzed again.

II

And the Spirits behind the curtains heard,
And also laughed, amused at her word,
And at her light-hearted view of him.
'Let's get him made so – just for a whim!'
Said the Phantom Ironic. ' 'Twould serve her right
If we coaxed the Will do to it some night.'
'O pray not!' pleaded the younger one,
The Sprite of the Pities. 'She said it in fun!'

III

But so it befell, whatever the cause,
That what she had called him he next year was;
And on such a night, when she lay elsewhere,
He, watched by those Phantoms, again sat there,
And gazed, as if gazing on far faint shores,
At the empty bed through the folding-doors
As he remembered her words; and wept
That she had forgotten them where she slept.

The Whitewashed Wall

Why does she turn in that shy soft way
    Whenever she stirs the fire,
And kiss to the chimney-corner wall,
    As if entranced to admire
Its whitewashed bareness more than the sight
    Of a rose in richest green?
I have known her long, but this raptured rite
    I never before have seen.

– Well, once when her son cast his shadow there,
    A friend took a pencil and drew him
Upon that flame-lit wall. And the lines
    Had a lifelike semblance to him.
And there long stayed his familiar look;
    But one day, ere she knew,
The whitener came to cleanse the nook,
    And covered the face from view.

'Yes,' he said: 'My brush goes on with a rush,
    And the draught is buried under;
When you have to whiten old cots and brighten,
    What else can you do, I wonder?'
But she knows he's there. And when she yearns
    For him, deep in the labouring night,
She sees him as close at hand, and turns
    To him under his sheet of white.

read more 🐧

PENGUIN RED CLASSICS

NORTH AND SOUTH
ELIZABETH GASKELL

'A wonderful love story' *Independent*

In a world of conflict, happiness can come in the most unexpected forms ...

Margaret's safe existence is turned upside down when her father dies and she has to move to the grim northern town of Milton. Not only does she have her eyes opened by the poverty and hardship she encounters there, but she is thrown into confusion by stern factory owner John Thornton – whose treatment of his workers brings them into fierce opposition.

As men and women, workers and masters come into violent conflict, it seems opposites can never meet. But do John and Margaret's power struggles hide deeper feelings? And, when it seems Margaret has lost everything, can she find the one thing she never expected?

'Dazzling ...Margaret is a woman of great integrity, verve and passion' *Independent*

'Remarkable' Joanna Trollope

For classic fiction, read Red

www.penguinclassics.com/reds

PENGUIN RED CLASSICS

WUTHERING HEIGHTS
EMILY BRONTË

'Passion and romance written like they ought to be' *Guardian*

In a house haunted by memories, the past is everywhere ...

As darkness falls, a man caught in a snowstorm is forced to shelter at the strange, grim house Wuthering Heights. It is a place he will never forget. There he will come to learn the story of Cathy: how she was forced to choose between her well-meaning husband and the dangerous man she had loved since she was young. How her choice led to betrayal and terrible revenge – and continues to torment those in the present. How love can transgress authority, convention, even death.

And how desire can kill.

'Unsurpassable ... I love it' Barbara Trapido

For classic fiction, read Red

www.penguinclassics.com/reds

He just wanted a decent book to read ...

Not too much to ask, is it? It was in 1935 when Allen Lane, Managing
Director of Bodley Head Publishers, stood on a platform at Exeter railway
station looking for something good to read on his journey back to London.
His choice was limited to popular magazines and poor-quality paperbacks –
the same choice faced every day by the vast majority of readers, few of
whom could afford hardbacks. Lane's disappointment and subsequent anger
at the range of books generally available led him to found a company – and
change the world.

*'We believed in the existence in this country of a vast reading public for intelligent
books at a low price, and staked everything on it'*
Sir Allen Lane, 1902–1970, founder of Penguin Books

The quality paperback had arrived – and not just in bookshops. Lane was
adamant that his Penguins should appear in chain stores and tobacconists,
and should cost no more than a packet of cigarettes.

Reading habits (and cigarette prices) have changed since 1935, but
Penguin still believes in publishing the best books for everybody to
enjoy. We still believe that good design costs no more than bad design,
and we still believe that quality books published passionately and responsibly
make the world a better place.

So wherever you see the little bird – whether it's on a piece of
prize-winning literary fiction or a celebrity autobiography, political tour
de force or historical masterpiece, a serial-killer thriller, reference book,
world classic or a piece of pure escapism – you can bet that it represents the
very best that the genre has to offer.

Whatever you like to read – trust Penguin.

read more
www.penguin.co.uk